MILE MARKER

MAKING THE MOST OF SPIRITUAL MOMENTS ALONG THE WAY.

A FAMILY GUIDE

NIC ALLEN
&
CHASE BAKER

WESTBOW
PRESS®
A DIVISION OF THOMAS NELSON
& ZONDERVAN

This book is a work of non-fiction. Unless otherwise noted, the author and the publisher make no explicit guarantees as to the accuracy of the information contained in this book and in some cases, names of people and places have been altered to protect their privacy.

WestBow Press books may be ordered through booksellers or by contacting:

WestBow Press
A Division of Thomas Nelson & Zondervan
1663 Liberty Drive
Bloomington, IN 47403
www.westbowpress.com
1 (866) 928-1240

All Scripture quotations, unless otherwise indicated, are taken from the Holy Bible, New International Version®, NIV®. Copyright ©1973, 1978, 1984, 2011 by Biblica, Inc.™ Used by permission of Zondervan. All rights reserved worldwide. www.zondervan.com The "NIV" and "New International Version" are trademarks registered in the United States Patent and Trademark Office by Biblica, Inc.™

ISBN: 978-1-9736-5807-8 (sc)
ISBN: 978-1-9736-5808-5 (hc)
ISBN: 978-1-9736-5806-1 (e)

Library of Congress Control Number: 2019903515

Print information available on the last page.

WestBow Press rev. date: 4/25/2019

CONTENTS

WELCOME TO MILEMARKER

MAKING THE MOST OF SPIRITUAL MOMENTS ALONG THE WAY.

You are on this page because God purposed in your life to make you responsible for someone else. Maybe multiple someones.

You are a parent.

Perhaps this is how you feel today: With God there are no accidents, but for you, pregnancy and parenthood came as a total shock. You are very thankful for gestation. It was God's gift of lead time allowing you to prep, yet you remain fully aware that nine years wouldn't have been enough time, much less nine months to get ready.

Not you?

Maybe you're on this page: Parenthood came after a long season of fervent prayer regarding infertility or years waiting for an adoptive match. You longed for this day, planned for this day, and it finally arrived. Every single detail was something you prayed over, poured over, and prepped for endlessly until the arrival of your long awaited child.

Still not quite you?

How about this: Pregnancy came easily, the old-fashioned way. The idea of parenting never brought on more than the average amount of panic. You're hopeful that every other age and stage of the childrearing process is just as textbook. Warning: the textbook clearly states there will be frequent twists, turns, and bumps along this journey. Easy conception in no way indicates an easy road to graduation.

No matter how you got here, you are here. A mom. A dad. An aunt, uncle or grandparent stepping in to serve in this incredibly vital role. And oh, what a role it is.

Parents are the single most important influence in a child's life throughout every stage.

Brace yourself! Parents are the single most important influence in a child's life throughout every stage. How's that for pressure? Even though your independent two-year-old or newly-licensed driver may not admit it, parents matter most. Your son or daughter needs you. Even when your toddler son is screaming, "I can do it myself," and when your preteen daughter is rolling her eyes and pushing your limits, they both still really need you.

Scary? Yes. Blessing? Also yes.

Consider the wild world of nature for a moment.

Snake moms abandon their eggs shortly after laying them.

Lizards, too, abandon their eggs to the wild, bearing no responsibility for hatching and/or raising their young.

Harp seal moms wean their young within the first two weeks and leave them alone on a length of floating ice to fend for themselves.

Pandas tend to have twins. Survival of the fittest in mind, they choose the child with the highest chance of survival and abandon the other.

People? We have far longer with our young before letting them loose. Even then, we hope for lifelong connections.

Unlike many species, a human parent's job doesn't end at birth. It really just begins.

God has purposed a powerful life-long relationship between you and your child. Pause for a moment and thank God for that. God has purposed a powerful life-long relationship between you and your child. Even in cases of abandonment or neglect, the influence of a parent is paramount. Your child's connection to you is the single most important connection he or she has for all of their developmental life.

That's why this journal exists. Even though eighteen years till adulthood boasts a far greater opportunity than the harp seal's yellowcoat [offspring, cub, kid] raising, it's going to fly by and feel like only a little more than that two week period before the ice cap launch.

So you purpose in your heart to make the most of every moment. You don't want to miss an instant. Then, you realize that "every moment" is a lot and you'll likely fail. So you take a deep breath and decide to make the most of the significant moments in your child's life.

excess of two hundred. Why? They took the wrong route. Too bad they didn't realize it sooner into the mistake. Pride and an overdose of male ego had prevented the use of GPS. A quick two hour journey doubled in length and became far more complicated as they humbled themselves and relied upon "Siri" for an alternate route.

Milemarkers tell you where you are. And if you're in the wrong place, they can even help you get where you need to be. Nothing screams the urgency of a milemarker like discovering how far you are off course when it's too late to do anything about it. That's the thing. It's never too late. This side of heaven, God has allowed chance after chance after chance to course-correct.

THE FARTHER YOU GET OFF COURSE,
TWO THINGS ARE TRUE:
- **the more time it takes to get back on track.**
- **the more fuel it takes to complete the journey.**

The milemarkers defined and detailed in this resource will help you chart your course and stay on track while you strive to make more of the significant moments along the way. The goal is to help you navigate time and provide fuel for the journey. Regardless of where you are starting with your kids, milemarker moments matter.

HOW TO USE THIS JOURNAL

This journal is yours to create. It will help you make the most of your parenting journey as you engage major milemarkers in the life of your child. Use this resource to help you imagine ways to celebrate, creating lasting impressions on your child, and reflecting on those memorable moments.

Each milemarker section includes the following:

1

INTRODUCTION. Enough said. This is an overview of the age and stage of development where each particular milemarker comes into view. It's a description of where you are in your journey and a set up to the other elements you'll uncover in each section.

BONUS: To spur creativity, we've included a GIFT/ EXPERIENCE IDEA GENERATOR in each introduction. Think of it like Pinterest, a spot to view and save good ideas you might want to copy, adapt, and utilize for your family. An example of how to mark and celebrate each milemarker is provided; however, the hope is that you'll be prompted along the way to generate ideas unique to your family experience.

2

DEVOTION. The devotions establish spiritual truths for each milemarker. Allow the scripture to guide you through these phases of life. In 2 Timothy 3:16 it says, "All Scripture is God-breathed and is useful for teaching, rebuking, correcting and training in righteousness…" If this is true, then why wouldn't we want our parenting to be driven by the very breath of God?

GUIDE. The guides provide helpful resources to navigate you through key parenting moments in the life of your child. One example is how a parent might guide a child or student through the salvation experience. This section provides starting points to have significant conversations with your child.

3

PROMPT. A journal prompt is exactly what it sounds like. They are designed to initiate creative writing for a specific milemarker. You can journal as much or as little as you want. Our recommendation: the more the better. Some journal prompts will guide you to reflect on specific milemarker celebrations. Others will focus on the joy/hurt you experience parenting through certain situations, and others on your own childhood. Consider what a great gift this is to pass on to your children one day!

4

APPENDIX: At the close of the six milemarker sections is a section for additional records. What plans are you making along the way? What additional elements do you want to remember? What pearls of wisdom do you want to be sure to pass? There are sections and questions to record those too, making each idea and experience you encounter along the way part of the milemarker journey you take and pass on to your child.

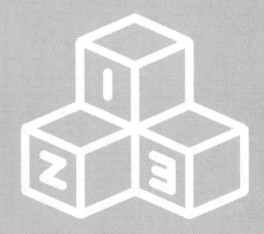

MILEMARKER 1

DEDICATION

INTRODUCTION TO
DEDICATION

God designed your child to grow. Every part of his or her anatomy and physiology was designed to operate in perfect harmony for the sole purpose of growth. Even when faced with significant special needs, the body's purpose is growth. As a parent, the key word for this stage is **"support"** *and it takes on two important meanings.*

First, your job isn't to create those biological systems but to support them. You don't digest and absorb the nutrients. You do, however, provide the food. You don't create neural pathways. You interact with your child to stimulate them. Simply put: You don't create the muscles that allow all the necessary movements for walking, but you do let your child grip your fingers when they take those first steps. This stage is about supporting the growth and development of your child - including spiritual growth. The way you talk about Jesus, engage the church, and bear fruit in your life will establish a tightly woven net to undergird your child's worldview long before they can articulate anything related to faith.

Next, in order to best support your child, you need support, too. "It takes a village." You need extended family and friends plus the love and support of your church community in order to raise a child well. Whatever goals you set in place for parenting will take a Spirit-filled team effort to achieve. Your support network will provide encouragement and strength to maintain faith during the journey. That network also assumes accompanying roles to help you demonstrate, articulate, and pass faith onto your child. Your support network also provides accountability. As you establish goals and guardrails to keep you on track, a strong, supportive community will prove providential.

QUESTIONS TO CONSIDER AS YOU NAVIGATE THIS STAGE?

- Who is my support system? Who can I best lean on?
- What guardrails will I set to keep me on track as an intentional parent?
- What spiritual goals will I make for myself that will directly impact my child? (prayer, Bible reading, service, etc…)
- What must I start doing to spend more time with my child?
- What should I stop doing to create more margin in my life for my child?

IDEA GENERATOR: Create a photo journal for the 1st birthday or church dedication service. Because the key word at this marker is "support," invite your network to script prayers and blessings. Paste the prayers and blessings with a photo of the person and make the journal a keepsake you can share with your child when they are older.

HANNAH [1 SAMUEL 1-2:11]

Hannah was barren. In today's terms, that was the Old Testament's equivalent of being uneducated and unemployed. Infertility didn't denote a medical reality but a community value. In Hannah's day, to be without a child [particularly a son] as a woman was to live without purpose for the present and also without hope for the future.

So Hannah did what believers do.

She prayed.

The message contained in Hannah's story could start and stop there. The act of depending on God for purpose, hope, value, worth, and life. Everyone could use that lesson. We all need a powerful reminder, at times, to point us in the only direction that matters. Trusting God in prayer. Peter exclaimed to Jesus, "Where else would we go? You alone have the words of eternal life!" [John 6:68] Hannah knew that. Where else would she go but to God?

So she found herself in the temple.

Earnest.

Heart sick.

She prayed for a child. It was a prayer for purpose-- purpose in being a mom; raising a son, a chance to carry on the promise of God to be fruitful and multiply, birthing one of the grains of sand in Abraham's family tree [Genesis 22:17]. She prayed a prayer for hope. Someone to love and someone to love her when she was old and widowed. She prayed to the only One who could provide.

Lesson learned. But the story went further still.

God answered and gave Hannah the son she desired. God gave her purpose. God gave her hope.

Samuel.

That wasn't the end of the story. Hannah responded by giving Samuel back to God. An act of worship. An act of obedience. A promise kept. Why?

Same scenario. Where else was she to go?

We give our children back to God because He alone is the source of life. Salvation is found in Him and Him alone. He is creator. He is also father. He is purpose giver and hope sustainer. Where else would we give our children? The dedication story of Hannah provides a framework for us as parents. We dedicate our children to the God who made them. We dedicate our children to the God who has purpose for them. We dedicate our children to the God who can give hope to them.

DEDICATING JESUS [LUKE 2:22-38]

If there was ever a child who did not need to be ceremonially dedicated, it was Jesus. Since the Jewish practice of dedicating a son included the covenant of circumcision, it was obviously necessary for the Christ child. However, when it came to the covenant blessing, dedicating Jesus, who was God, back to God, seems redundant right?

In observance of God's words to Israel in Exodus 13, the firstborn male in every family was to be dedicated/consecrated/set apart. The purpose was holiness. Ultimately, the word holy means "sanctified for special use." The "special use" intended for Jesus? Sacrifice. Never could there be a more appropriate action for a parent. To dedicate their child to God, his young parents, set him [who had once set them] apart for special use...sacrificial use within God's Kingdom.

The dedicated Jesus was named "salvation," by the prophet Simeon.

The dedicated Jesus was welcomed with worship, fasting, and prayer by the Prophetess Anna.

The dedicated Jesus was one with His Father in purpose and power. Why? Because when Mary and Joseph brought Jesus to be dedicated, Scripture says that Jesus came "in the Spirit." The same Spirit with Him at creation. The same Spirit present who overshadowed Mary at conception. The same Spirit who would descend at Jesus' baptism. The same Spirit who would lead Jesus into the wilderness. The same Spirit, who Jesus would one day promise to fill believers at Pentecost.

That same Spirit of God was moving in Luke 2. Alive. Active. Living. Present with Jesus at dedication.

Jesus was always one with His father, filled with the Spirit, pointing believers to complete communion with God. How? By the Spirit. Jesus was dedicated to His Father in spirit and dedicated to serve His Father by His earthly parents. It's this model we follow and this communion we long for when we dedicate our own kids, too.

PRAYING AS A PARENT

> Oswald Chambers famously penned,
> *"Prayer does not fit us for the greater works;*
> *prayer is the greater work."*

When a nose is runny, the must-have quick-fix is a simple tissue, preferably one with a little lotion or aloe to avoid the dry-cracked burning sensation that comes with over-blowing.

How about a banged-up knee? Antibacterial ointment and a bandage, and perhaps a little freezer pal [boo-boo bunny], will do the trick.

BE ADVISED: Both aforementioned parenting tricks would also benefit from a little cuddling, too.

Parents like to fix things. We want to solve problems. Eliminate germs. Dry tears. Prevent falls and spills and even leave margin for turning frowns upside down.

When it comes to parenting, so much of the daily responsibilities are in the "do" column. They are tangible actions, problem-solving techniques, and small investments to yield almost immediate results.

Prayer often makes its way into the "do" column although we sometimes fail to experience the immediate results we'd like. We believe in its power and we know it's good and right so we "do" prayer, missing the reality that prayer is far more about who you are rather than what you do.

Over the life of your child, it is crucial that you pray for and also with him or her. It matters that you pray. It is better still if prayer just becomes another part of who you are as a parent. Here are a few book recommendations if you'd like to dive deeper into the concept of praying over your children.

- *Praying Circles Around the Lives of Your Children* - **Mark Batterson**
- *The Power of a Praying Parent* - **Stormie Omartian**

When it comes to ideas, the Bible isn't short on admonitions to pray and even grand examples of prayer. Praying scripture over your children is a fantastic practice to include. This might sound a little counter productive, but before you can pray for your child, you really must pray for his or her parents.

"Wait? Doesn't that mean I'll be praying for myself?" you might ask.

Yes. It does. Here's why:

Airlines.

Airlines?

Yes. Airlines.

What does the flight attendant say when she models careful use of the face mask that drops should the cabin lose pressure? She reminds those of us traveling with minors or others needing assistance to put on our masks first. Why? Because you are no good to your child if you are passed out due to lack of oxygen. Like the air you need to breathe, you need the Holy Spirit's power to parent your child.

As a praying parent, you will pray for your child's health, safety, purpose, beliefs, education, friendships, heart, sin, attitude, effort, opportunities, future, and so much more.

Be sure to also take time to pray for yourself as your child's mom or dad. Why? Because having a mom or dad who loves and follows Jesus will do immeasurably more for your child's health, safety, education, purpose, beliefs, education, friendships, heart, sin, attitude, effort, opportunities, and future than you can imagine.

A few ideas to get started:

+ **Pray** that you will be a parent with godly priorities.

+ **Pray** that you will be a parent with margin and space in your life for real relationships.

+ **Pray** that you will model healthy eating, exercise, and good sleep patterns.

+ **Pray** that you will fill your cup daily with God's word and your child will notice it and mimic it.

+ **Pray** that God will protect your eyes and hands from sin and temptation.

+ **Pray** that your relationships will be holy and Christ-centered.

+ **Pray** for opportunities to take risks, be missional, and share Jesus with others.

+ **Pray** for provision and also for faithful, generous giving to be modeled in your home.

+ **Pray** that Jesus would be Lord of your whole life and that it would be evidenced by the fruit you bear.

+ **Pray** that the habits your child picks up from you will drive them closer to Christ.

+ **Pray** that whatever mistakes you make along the way will ultimately be leveraged for God's glory and grace.

"NO ONE HAS MORE POTENTIAL TO INFLUENCE YOUR CHILD THAN YOU."

REGGIE JOINER,
PARENTING BEYOND YOUR CAPACITY
[Orange Books, 2015]

In comic book Superhero narratives, we call them "origin stories." The infant, Kal-El from planet Krypton, came to earth in a spaceship and was raised as Clark Kent. Who did he eventually become? Superman. The word nativity literally means "the occasion of a person's birth." The most famous nativity, of course, is that of Jesus. Everyone has a nativity or origin story, including your child. For this journal entry, compose your child's origin story. It's one that they can read and understand later in life. Maybe their birth story includes issues with fertility, an early arrival, or an eventful delivery. Through this entry, your child will have a keepsake narrative of how and when they came to be.

_____

_____

_____

_____

_____

_____

_____

_____

_____

_____

Nine months is both long and short. Waiting for your child's arrival may seem simultaneously like the blink of an eye and a day that would never come. During pregnancy, you prayed many prayers for your child. For his or her health. For his or her development. For his or her future. Read Psalm 139:13-16. God knows all the days of your child's life. In this journal, script a special prayer for your child. Jot down thoughts of hope for his or her salvation and discipleship. Include prayers and dreams for wisdom, pursuit of holiness, and your child's ability to find joy in Christ no matter what circumstances occur in life. Even include prayer for yourself to best love, nurture, guide, and protect in the manner Christ is calling you.

_____

_____

_____

_____

_____

_____

_____

_____

_____

_____

_____

_____

_____

_____

_____

_____

_____

_____

_____

_____

_____

_____

_____

_____

_____

_____

_____

MILEMARKER 2

EDUCATION

INTRODUCTION TO EDUCATION

Your child has been learning since they first opened their eyes and drew breath. Since the first cry, they have been in constant information mode. Starting formal schooling in kindergarten could seem anticlimactic considering the vast amount of education your child has already digested in the first five years of life. However, there is a transition taking place, one that starts an amazing journey. If a high school student opts to continue, twelve years of required education can quickly become 16, 18 or even 20 years of school. That is a significant portion of life. No matter the credentials, no one values your child's education in the manner that you do.

The key word during this phase is "**discovery**." One of the duties you assume during this phase is to protect your child's sense of curiosity in order to prolong it. There will be things along the way that will stifle a child's love for learning. Deciding how you to establish boundaries and provide encouragement will matter. There are exceptions, but in large part, your child will learn to value learning to the degree that you do. If he senses that you place a high value on performance, his perceptions of learning will be tainted. Setting the tone for learning, education, and discovery being powerful ends unto themselves will aid your child for the long haul. It will also further till the soil where faith seeds are daily being planted.

Because it's easier to set long term education goals with college and career in mind, parents may limit the focus they lend to biblical education and the role of faith in childhood development. As a parent, it's up to you to prioritize scripture during these years so your son or daughter doesn't wake up one day with a warped perception of the Bible's prominent role in life. There is a difference between intelligence and wisdom. As your child enters the education phase of life, he will take his cues about both, first, from you.

QUESTIONS TO CONSIDER AS YOU NAVIGATE THIS PHASE:

- What type of formal education opportunities do you prefer for your child?
- What were the key positive and negative characterizations of your formal education experience?
- In what ways do you learn? What sparks your sense of curiosity and discovery?
- In what ways can you spark deeper curiosity and discovery in your child's knowledge of God and His word?
- What stifles learning for you and also for your child?
- Do you know the teachers, small group leaders, pastors, and coaches that teach your child?

IDEA GENERATOR: At this milemarker, consider the rhythms you establish. A respite retreat to the mountains over fall break. Celebrating academic achievements at the conclusion of a school year. Memorizing bible verses and passages together as a family. Missional acts of service over spring break. Summer holiday celebrations. Time really is one of the greatest gifts you can give your kids. Individually, these experiences of time spent together can be so special. Repeated and cultivated year after year, they become traditions that frame your child's sense of discovery.

These experiences create the vocabulary your son or daughter will use to describe their formative years. The best idea at this phase is to generate a few simple, yet good, ideas you are able to repeat as a family rhythm for the years ahead. Create a family rhythm calendar together, marking all the moments of exploration and celebration that frame your year.

FAITH ALONG THE WAY

*Hear, O Israel: The L*ORD *our God, the L*ORD *is one. Love the L*ORD *your God with all your heart and with all your soul and with all your strength. These commandments that I give you today are to be on your hearts. Impress them on your children. Talk about them when you sit at home and when you walk along the road, when you lie down and when you get up. Tie them as symbols on your hands and bind them on your foreheads. Write them on the doorframes of your houses and on your gates.*[**DEUTERONOMY 6:4-9**]

Along the way. That's a foundational truth in the walk of a believer in Jesus. And the concept dates back to the beginning of the covenant relationship between Israel and Yahweh. Now, coming up on the tail end of their wilderness experience, God, through Moses, reminds the people of His priority seat in their lives and sets His Word and Will in the context of that idea…along the way.

Verse 4 in this passage is really important. It's known as the *"shema"* and serves as the foundational confession of faith in God for the Jew. When it comes to God the Father through Jesus the Son by the power of the Spirit being of singular importance in our lives today, it's a foundational confession for us, too. When Christ was asked by the attorney, aka legal expert, to name the most important command, Jesus quoted Deuteronomy 6:5. [See Luke 10:25-27] Jesus wasn't even paraphrasing and clarifying a summarized interpretation of the Old Testament law. He simply named the most important command. It was such that any God-fearing Jew in Jesus' Palestine, especially the Pharisee conducting the interview, would have known by memory.

Moses followed up that primary statute with a very strategic plan to pass faith on to future generations.

Repeat them to your kids.

Make it part of everyday conversation around the house and as you travel.

Strategically place the ideals of loving God and following His Word first and last in each day. When you wake up. When you turn in. Make the value of knowing, loving, and following God evident--visible in your life--like jewelry on your hand or on your head. Attach it to your doors. Not the legendary rock band fronted by poetic lyricist Jim Morrison, but the actual entryway into your home or place of business. God instructed people to display His Word on the entrance to their homes. It would be the first thing someone saw when entering and the last thing they viewed upon leaving.

Several things stand out about this final inclusion regarding doors in God's generational faith-passing strategy. First, people who are camping out don't have doors. Second, writing words is far easier than painting blood. Maybe not easier. But much cleaner. The last time Israel had doors, they also had hyssop. And they obeyed God by using hyssop to paint the blood of a sacrificed lamb around the door frame. That blood protected first born kids from physical death and destruction. Now, it was written words that were to be on the doors, written words that would protect kids, this time from spiritual death and destruction.

Israel was entering a land to possess and cities they didn't build. To drink from wells they didn't dig. To enjoy harvest they didn't plant. To live in full houses they didn't fill. With doors! [See Deuteronomy 6:10-11]

The challenge with displaying God's word visibly in your home is pretty obvious. Owning a hammer doesn't make you a carpenter anymore than owning a Bible makes you a theologian. Just because you frame God's word doesn't mean you follow it. We all benefit from reminders, though. Ultimately, Deuteronomy 6 was review. God had given Israel an intense law that could easily be summed up by one phrase, "Love Him." Deuteronomy 6 was a reminder to put God first, not just when your life is in a wilderness but also when you occupy the land.

Must we literally display God's word in our homes? Not necessarily, but consider this: By not displaying God's word on a doorway or around your home, do we run the risk of forgetting to display it in our lives as well? Does it further the chance we might raise kids who don't get it, who are more like Judges 2:10 than they are Exodus 24:3. Check out the difference:

JUDGES 2:10 "That whole generation was also gathered to their ancestors. After them another generation rose up who did not know the Lord or the works He had done for Israel."

EXODUS 24:3 "Moses came and told the people all the commands of the Lord and all the ordinances. Then all the people responded with a single voice, 'We will do everything that the Lord has commanded.'"

On stone tablets, only God could script His word. On our homes, He asks us to hold the pen. Repetition and reminders matter to God. They matter to our kids, too, if we are to strategically pass faith. At the first passover, hyssop was the prescribed tool for painting blood. Now, scripture is the essential tool for passing faith. And when we talk about scripture early in the morning and before bed each night, around the table and to-and-fro, we're far more apt to pass it fully and prevent them from forgetting. Is it that rigid a recipe? Do you need a spreadsheet with tick-marks every time you talk about God? No. But you do need to cultivate conversations about the Lord all along the way.

God doesn't ask us today to hue our houses in the blood of an animal. It would take the strongest of stomachs to be an Old Testament priest. God has asked us, however, to write His words on our homes and in our hearts. This journey is all about doing that in such a way that our kids don't miss it. We desire kids who love God, trust Christ, and live by the Spirit. We know that we can't manufacture that.

It's God's word that offers protection, provides purpose, and preserves his perfect presence in our lives. It's also the manner in which we live out those distinct lives we're called to enjoy in the land. Disorder and destruction are the byproducts of ignoring God's word. Those dangerous outcomes also manifest when we allow Scripture to take a back seat among the myriad of other options we have in everyday life. May we all cling to the reminders He gives and the ones we desperately need, to ensure God's presence and prominence in our lives and definitely in the lives of our kids.

FAMILY DEVOTIONAL MOMENTS

GO BIG OR GO HOME, RIGHT? Who doesn't want kids who can recite the entire book of 1 John and carry on great conversations about soteriology and defend their faith in God?

Slow down. That isn't the purpose of your family's devotional time or even a very realistic goal for it. The purpose of your family's devotional life is to create space for the Holy Spirit, reinforce your family's commitment to Jesus, and worship the living God together. One day, that might include catechism and scripture memory attached to important doctrinal truths.

Side note: catechism is making a comeback. Formerly attached to more traditional protestant denominations, it's a series of questions and answers that define and summarize basic Christian principles. It's becoming more prevalent in modern evangelical conversations and there are great resources to aid the process. Even still, raising kids who can recite and repeat isn't the purpose of your devotional life. It may be a fantastic means towards a wonderful byproduct but it's not the overall end goal.

Why have a family devotion? The answer here is merely the plural of why you should have a personal or private devotion. To cultivate a growing relationship with God where you worship and practice spiritual disciplines like prayer, fasting, and scripture reading. It's space every day to interact with God's word and draw closer to Him. The same will be true for a family who devotes such time together. So what constitutes a family devotional time? That varies based on the age and stage of your children.

PRESCHOOLERS: You might read one or two verses or choose to employ the use of an illustrated story-based Bible like the *Jesus Storybook Bible* by Sally Lloyd-Jones. You can sing a song, recognize and pray for family members and a missionary. By that point, attention spans have long since expired. The goal is to make devotional time a natural part of the rhythm and weekly routine of your home.

ELEMENTARY: You may expand scripture readings and even include young readers. You may also select a devotional book to follow like *Jesus Calling for Kids* by Sarah Young. You can continue to sing a song together and even expand your playlist. Worship songs in so many genres are easily accessible. Continuing praying for family members, missionaries, and personally for one another. Doctrinal truths and Christian principles can really begin to take shape. Researching a catechism resource for kids might be just what your family needs. Check out "The New City Catechism" by Kathy Keller.

MIDDLE AND HIGH SCHOOL: This is the phase of life when schedules can really upset the apple cart. The priority here is just that--priority. Does driving to and from soccer replace devotion? Hopefully not, if the practice is established. Flexibility is key to sustainability. At this stage, start reading Christian classics and using more mature devotionals like modern interpretations of *My Utmost for His Highest* by Oswald Chambers or Sarah Young's *Jesus Always*. Begin a family Bible reading plan together. Numerous options are available on YouVersion. The likelihood of smart devices and social media creates opportunities to leverage technological resources for family devotional good.

Don't forget! Your family devotional moments will only be blessed in conjunction with your dedication to personal devotional moments. A car doesn't run on empty. A parent doesn't run on empty, either. Reading a few verses with your children and praying as a family can supplement your own spiritual growth, but not sustain your overall spiritual health. You need personal, devotional disciplines and a community of faith among other adults you are learning from and growing alongside. You don't just influence your child's spiritual growth by what you do with them but also by what you model for them. The devotional life your son or daughter adopts will employ things they learn from the family environment you cultivate but also, maybe more so, the devotional life you personally live in front of them.

> You don't just influence your child's spiritual growth by what you do with them but also by what you model for them.

BEGINNING THE SEX TALK

> *Look around. It's everywhere.*
> S-E-X.

Not just sex. Sexuality. Sexual tension. Sexual exploitation. Sexual identity and subsequent sexual identity crises. Culture doesn't just address the issue once. Culture engages sex constantly. Long gone are the days when moms and dads could count on one simple "birds and bees" conversation to provide all the necessary elements to raise a healthy son or daughter. FYI: those days never existed and proper research might even reveal that we are where we are today because parents, in generations gone by, thought one easy [also awkward] metaphor would suffice.

The way to begin the sex talk with your kids in preschool and elementary school is to recognize several important factors.

1. OWN YOUR OWN SEXUAL HISTORY. It's a far bigger piece of the puzzle than a simple bullet on this list. As you plan to talk about sex and sexuality with your child, it's important to reconcile your own sexual past. We all have mistakes in this area of life, mistakes we hope our kids will learn from and avoid. You are not ready to talk about any of that with your child until you have first talked about it with the Lord, your spouse, and even a trusted friend or counselor who can help you navigate the effects of how past sins have scarred your life. Do some careful exploration in this area as you consider the route you plan to take with these conversations.

2. ONE CONVERSATION WILL NOT SUFFICE.

As a parent, you want to secure the position of expert authority. You are the encyclopedia of sexuality you want your children to read. Not TV. Not social media. Not song lyrics. Not your neighbor down the street or the older kid on the bus. Engagement is how you earn that role. Awareness and approachability when your child has questions are how you maintain that spot.

3. YOU MUST START EARLY.

The sex talk doesn't begin with reproduction but with bodies being uniquely and wonderfully made by God. It includes anatomy and modesty. Certain parts of our bodies must remain covered and untouched by others. The sex talk begins with teaching children that their bodies are special, made by God, and not to be abused. It matters that your children know the difference between safe touches and unsafe ones. This lays the groundwork for future sex talks.

4. YOU NEED OUTSIDE SOURCES.

Books, ministries, counselors, pastors, and small group leaders. Even friends with children who have navigated these seas before will come in handy. It is important that you remain the most important voice in your child's life but that you also recruit other trustworthy voices. You can never be the only voice in your child's life. If you want your future 14-year-old daughter to trust her 8th grade small group leader, foster that relationship by making her 2nd grade small group a priority. If she learns the value of discipleship at a young age and you affirm her participation in a group where someone can pour into her life while you are still more than enough, she'll already have that framework established when you are no longer all she needs.

Little conversations along the way establish trust for the big ones later on. You want to create a balance between intentionally starting the conversations and waiting to answer questions when your child asks. This journey will require both. Questions will come at inopportune times and they could be shocking. Breathing deep, being calm, and at least appearing to be prepared will continue to foster the confidence your child will need to trust you and make wise choices along the way. It won't only be about the questions, though. You'll need to carve out time for intentionally scripted educational moments. Just like starting school or trusting Jesus as Savior, these conversations are developmental milestones that paint a bigger picture and write a better story for your child.

HOW TO CREATE MISSIONAL DNA

Traits, qualities, and features that characterize a person or thing...DNA. In other words, the makeup of our bodies. Every person has a DNA completely different than anyone else. That is pretty amazing!

But when we talk about Missional DNA, we are still talking about traits, qualities, and features that characterize a body--the Body of Christ.

1 Corinthians 12:12
"Just as a body, though one, has many parts, but all its many parts form one body, so it is with Christ."

We are in this together and every single one of us who makes up the Body of Christ is connected to the same Missional DNA.

Jesus said, "Go, therefore, and make disciples." The word "go" literally means, "as you go" or "as you are going." When Jesus gave this command, His intention was that we express His love in every facet of our lives, not just the parts of our lives associated with church. To have a missional DNA, we must understand what mission we are on: God's mission. to redeem all people by the saving grace He offers through Jesus' death, burial, and resurrection. Our mission, in turn, is simple: to love the world as God has loved the people in it, bringing Him glory and pointing others to a saving relationship with Him through Jesus Christ.

40

This section of the book is about processing and understanding the missional DNA of children when they become Christ followers. It's a process that necessitates intentionality in every aspect of life.

Instilling a missional DNA in the life of a child will:

- **TEACH SACRIFICE.** How many times have you heard the phrases... "It's MINE," "Give it to ME," or "I want?" In a society that focuses on "ME," a missional DNA shines a light on others.

- **CHANGE LANGUAGE OVER TIME.** We speak to the degree we have been spoken to. Changing the me-centered language happens within family interactions over time. Actions directly correlate to words we use in daily conversation. Therefore, the use of language and the development of vocabulary is essential to the missional DNA of your family. What gets talked about gets done.

- **BROADEN BIBLICAL WORLDVIEW.** A worldview is the framework in which we view reality and make sense of the world around us. A person's ideology, philosophy, opinions, or religion will ultimately establish how a child understands the world and how they will interact with the people around them. Therefore, a biblical worldview is based on the Word of God. Your child's worldview will constantly be bombarded with television, film, music, news, magazines, social media, and academics. You can't assume their worldview is being fully shaped by the Bible from a 1-2 hour bible study at church, even with perfect weekend attendance. We have an opportunity to shape the worldview of our children through the lens of the Bible, ultimately leading to LOVE and SACRIFICE.

- **CHALLENGE TO ACTIVATE FAITH.** Nothing can replace learning through experience. Some of the most impacting experiences your son or daughter will remember and reflect on as a young adult will likely be those when he or she was pushed outside of a proverbial comfort zone and put in a place to serve others missionally. It's precisely those situations when we learn how to see the needs of others and are challenged to meet those needs. Those are the moments when we hear stories and understand people better, when we discover what everyday faith can look like as we seek to sacrificially honor God. This doesn't happen from the sidelines. When we continue to challenge our children and provide opportunities to serve, we WILL create a missional DNA.

- **DRIVE THEM TO LOVE.** Ultimately, this is the goal, right? To raise a generation that will understand Jesus' words when He said, "By this everyone will know that you are my disciples, if you love one another." (John 13:35) LOVE draws us to a saving relationship with God. Only to the degree that we value and understand that same love will we be driven to live our lives engaging the mission of God.

So where do we begin?

Start Daily. "Missional Living" isn't a single season like fall soccer or summer swim team. It requires an emphasis on teaching, coaching, and modeling every single day. Simply accepting that this is a day-to-day lifestyle and not an annual focus will help build a solid foundation for kids before they move into various stages of responsibility as they get older. This attitude of daily sacrifice starts in the home among family and friends.

Serve in your local church. Long term goal alert: You want to raise a child who knows and understands how he or she fits within the Body of Christ. Look for ways to invest in your local church. Help your child discover their gifts and how they can use those gifts to build up the church body. Help them know and understand they serve an awesome God who has created them, uniquely, in order to give back. Demonstrate to your children the value of serving in both the areas of their greatest gifts and passions and also the greatest needs within the life of your church.

Move to a family LOCAL MISSION experience. Find a ministry within your local church or a non-profit organization with which to volunteer. After you serve, ask intentional questions and create conversation. "Why do you think it is important for our family to serve?" "Why would God want us to help people?" "Do you think we honored God today?"

Someone might say that living "on mission" isn't something you schedule. It's simply the overflow who you are. That may be true, but it doesn't begin there. For sacrificial living to become natural in your child, it must be modeled for and scheduled with your child throughout their journey of discovery.

"DO YOU KNOW THAT NOTHING YOU DO IN LIFE WILL EVER MATTER, UNLESS IT IS ABOUT LOVING GOD & LOVING THE PEOPLE HE HAS MADE?"

FRANCIS CHAN CRAZY LOVE,
OVERWHELMED BY A RELENTLESS GOD
[David. C. Cook, 2015]

*Sean Covey, son of Stephen Covey, followed his dad's best selling book **The Seven Habits of Highly Effective People** with his own version titled **The Seven Habits of Highly Effective Teens**. He wrote, "We become what we repeatedly do." Ultimately, that's what a habit is. Take time in this journal entry to list the habits you hope will characterize your son or daughter as they grow and learn. These are the very habits that should characterize your life, as well. After each habit, note the ways you currently are or intend to begin cultivating that particular habit.*

_____

_____

_____

_____

_____

_____

_____

_____

_____

_____

_____

_____

_____

_____

Imagine giving your child the story of your own educational journey as a keepsake? What subjects did you love and which ones did you merely endure? How did you know what path to take and what educational direction would be included in your life? Did you choose higher education? Why or why not? What factors were at play with your choice of vocation? Who influenced you along the way? What prayers are you praying for your child's education, direction, and future? Also include the role God played in your choices and pursuits. Express your hope for Christ's influence in your child's decisions as he or she grows and learns.

_____

_____

_____

_____

_____

_____

_____

_____

_____

_____

_____

MILEMARKER 3

SALVATION

INTRODUCTION TO SALVATION

You will experience no greater joy as a parent than witnessing your child's conversion to Christ. You may feel a sense of undue responsibility or anxiety regarding your child's decision to trust Jesus as Savior. While the other milemarker celebrations are age and stage specific, salvation can come at any point in the journey as long as the child is old enough to understand and reconcile concepts like sin and sacrifice.

The key word during this stage is "**forgiveness**." Salvation itself is easy enough for a child to comprehend but complicated enough to keep us studying, reading, and wrestling for a lifetime. As a parent helping your son or daughter navigate this decision, keep coming back to that key word, "forgiveness," and this key concept: the difference between needs and wants. Salvation is ultimately, in base form, a transaction of substitutionary atonement. Sinners are separated from God by sin [not just the wrongs we commit but the very nature of who we are]. Good works cannot make up for the wrong we do and the very core of who we are. Atonement must be made to pay for those wrongs and reconcile who we are before God.

In Christianity, that atonement has been made by a suitable substitute. The temporary lamb or goat of the Old Testament became the permanent once and for all Savior of the New Testament, Jesus Christ [God's only Son] Himself. His death purchased our forgiveness.

Once your child can recite the details of the Easter story and express the desire to become a Christian, it can be simple to celebrate and bypass actual comprehension. That's where parental discernment comes into play. As a mom or dad, you understand the difference between needs and wants. A new board game is different than a balanced diet. One is a need and the other, a want. A child may *want* to become a Christian for a variety of reasons at each stage of development. Until a child understands the *need* to become a Christian, he or she isn't quite ready. Wanting to follow Jesus is an important part of the equation but it's not the only necessary part. Understanding and articulating his or her sin before God and dire need for His special forgiveness is the necessary factor. When your child is ready, he or she will be able to say with confidence, in some form or another, that Christ died in our place because we are desperate sinners in need of forgiveness in order to stand clean before God. No matter the verbiage, "forgiveness" is the key word and understanding our need for it is the key concept to experience salvation from sin and freedom in Christ.

As a parent or primary parental figure, no one is in a better position to influence that decision than you. For the parent raising their child in the church, this can mean that even young children declare their faith in Christ early before they fully understand the sacrifice He made. It means your child's salvation experience will be marked as a long developmental journey and not a one-time u-turn decision. It means you won't have one conversation with your child about salvation but countless ones cultivated over time, sowing seeds of faith that last.

QUESTIONS TO CONSIDER AS
YOU NAVIGATE THIS STAGE:

- What is my salvation story or personal testimony?
- Have I demonstrated salvation through my own believer's baptism experience?
- Who shaped and influenced my knowledge of Jesus and salvation?
- Who is actively influencing my son or daughter to know and follow Jesus?
- Is my parenting style helping my child better understand the rules of God or the grace of God?
- Is my child ready to take the next step to experience salvation and follow Jesus?
- What is next for my son or daughter in their discipleship process?
- How can I emphasize the need for baptism as a spiritually symbolic marker and not identify baptism as the regenerate act that saves a person?

IDEA GENERATOR: As a symbol of salvation, God gave us the gift of baptism. It's important to note, at this juncture, that believer's baptism differs from infant baptism because of the repentance of the believer. It indicates a person turning to and trusting Christ. Believer's baptism is an outward expression of an inward transformation. As you prepare to celebrate baptism with your child, consider the gifts you may give to mark the occasion. A keepsake Bible, personal devotional, or prayer journal are all great ideas. Something special like a locket, cross pendant, framed photo from the baptism, or a custom art print of a special life verse or scripture passage would also serve as wonderful milemarker reminders. Whatever you choose, make it unique to your child. Be sure to include a handwritten letter to your son or daughter celebrating the occasion and indicating your joy over their decision to trust and follow Jesus.

BAPTISM OF JESUS [MATTHEW 3]

Ever wonder why we call baptism a public profession of faith? In the water, the person being baptized does a few significant things:

1. They wordlessly declare the saving faith of the gospel. The act of going in the water and being baptized in the name of the Father, Son, and Holy Spirit in view of whatever witnesses present is a symbolic declaration of the belief in Christ that saves a sinner.

2. They symbolically describe God's plan of redemption. Sin separates man from God. Through the atoning sacrifice of Jesus, man's sins can be forgiven [removed and made clean]. While the water itself is neither cleansing or salvific, the act of going in and coming out illustrates the washing away of sin.

3. They effectively tell the story of Jesus. Sinless Christ was crucified unto death, buried in a tomb, but raised to life again. Immersion paints that same picture for the believer. Pastors may even recite, "buried with him in baptism, raised to walk in a new life." The simple act of baptism illustrates the manner in which salvation came.

4. Finally, they indicate repentance and identify publicly as a follower of Jesus. As John baptized Jews and Gentiles, it was an outward sign of an inward repentance and a demarcation of followership. To be baptized by John meant a person now followed the teachings of John. To be

baptized in the name of Jesus, telling His gospel story, celebrates one as a Christ follower.

Something significant happened when Jesus came out of the water. We find in Matthew 3:16-17 a perfect picture of the Holy Trinity.

+ Jesus came out of the water.

+ The Holy Spirit descended from the opened heavens as a dove.

+ The Father spoke, "This is My Beloved Son, with whom I am well pleased."

We celebrate believer's baptism in our churches today to follow the example of Jesus and obey the Bible's command. This simple but public profession is one of many ways the true believer in Jesus confesses Christ before men and declares His sole hope in Jesus for all eternity. Just as God the Father made His public declaration about the messianic validity of Jesus following His baptism, immersed believers make their public profession of Jesus. He is truly God's son, in whom we are made pleasing to God.

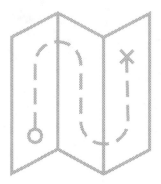

GUIDING YOUR CHILD THROUGH THE SALVATION EXPERIENCE

The conversations you have about salvation in your home are the most important you'll ever have. There are some necessary disclaimers to get you started.

1. START EARLY. The goal isn't just a one time presentation to seal the deal. It's also not wise to wait until your child is old enough to ask questions and consider the abstract principles related to Lordship before beginning. Salvation, like so much else in life, starts with story. Begin with the story of Jesus from day one so that when your child is old enough to engage, the framework is already in place.

2. REPEAT OFTEN. You'll continue to help your child understand [warning: big word coming up soon] soteriology for the remainder of your life. Soteriology is the doctrine of salvation. Even how you process and approach aging and eventually death, will influence your son or daughter's doctrine of salvation. According to Philippians 2, salvation is something we will always continue to work out, wrestle with, and understand better. Your conversations will not begin at any certain age, nor will they discontinue when your child has trusted Jesus and been baptized.

3. BREATHE DEEP. If there is any part of you that feels the weight of talking about this important subject, good! You should feel the burden of this important topic, but not so much that you are paralyzed and frozen with fear. You are an awesome parent. Seriously. You are. Just being willing to engage important matters is half the battle. Now, the other half is what you do with the knowledge you acquire. Seriously, just entering the conversation and to grow as a parent is awesome. So, way to go!

The big overarching goal is always spiritual transformation. The kind that only comes from a real encounter with Christ. It's the result of the gospel. When you hear the word gospel, we're not just talking about the first four books of the New Testament – gospel literally means "good news" and it includes all of scripture. We're talking about the story of God start to finish. It was certainly made complete by the story of Jesus presented in Matthew, Mark, Luke, and John but without the narrative of the Old Testament and the exposition of the remaining parts of the New, we wouldn't even know why Jesus coming was good news. So when we write "gospel," we mean the entire good news story of scripture.

Spiritual transformation comes from an encounter with Christ as a result of the gospel story changing a person's life.

We were all on a dangerous road because of sin, a road that leads to death and eternal separation from God. The gospel puts you on a different road entirely, one that leads to eternal life in Christ. Leaving no room for confusion or doubt, Christ is the only way.

How can any of this transformation apply to kids? Go back to the road illustration. Picture a really long highway, something like Interstate 40 from California to North Carolina. Imagine someone leaves Wilmington, and heads west at 3 a.m. one Monday morning. It's now

6pm, 18 hours later, they are halfway to Barstow. Say someone leaves Wilmington and heads west at 4pm in the afternoon. Dinner time rolls around and they've barely made it to Raleigh. It's the same road with the same destination but way less coverage.

Sin is a road that always only leads to death. You can be on that road for 18 years or 18 minutes but the destination is exactly the same. Spiritual transformation is what gets you off that dangerous road. And it comes from a realization of what sin is and a belief in what Christ did.

Someone who trusts Jesus for salvation as an older adult has traveled the road of sin for a much longer time period and has certainly gone a far greater distance, but connecting with the gospel got them off of that road. A child may not have been very far down that road before experiencing that same gospel and getting off that course.

As parents, that is our goal. Horace Bushnell (wouldn't you like to be named Horace Bushnell!) said that we should raise our kids in such a way that they never remember not being a Christian. [Christian Nurture, Scribner & Sons, 1908] He lived over 120 years ago and he was called a heretic, but he was right. His work is now regarded highly within Christian education. Our goal as parents should be to raise our kids to know Christ, hoping and praying that they will grow up not remembering a time when they did not know and believe in God.

The questions then become, for a lot of us, what does it take to make sure that my child is a Christian? What are the steps? What is it that they have to know and believe? When are they ready?

The short answer is, as a believer and a parent filled with the spirit of God, you know when you know.

The longer answer is really just a few key points of understanding that we think kids should know and be able to articulate. Not just in a "I know the right answer in my head" kind of way, but in a "my life is really shaped and formed by this understanding" kind of way. It does have to be a *heart* knowledge.

1. FIRST, SIN – without a concept of sin, we don't need forgiveness. Without the need for forgiveness, Christ died for nothing, and the gospel is pointless. Here's the basis of what a child, or anyone coming to Jesus, needs to know about sin. It's not just the list of don'ts or the bad stuff we do. It's ultimately who we are as fallen creatures. It is what separates us from God. It means we can't have a relationship with Him. It defines us. Whether we make one mistake or 1,000 every day, we are still the same dirty, rotten sinners and we don't deserve God's love. Understanding sin is the difference between, "I want to be a Christian" and "I need to be a Christian." Anyone can want to follow the teaching of Jesus. Only a true believer, transformed by grace, knows how desperately they need Jesus.

2. WHICH BRINGS US TO THE NEXT KEY POINT OF UNDERSTANDING – JESUS. What must a person know, believe, and understand about Jesus? He is God made flesh. In kid language, that means that He is totally God and was here before creation, but at the right time, took human form as a child, God's very own son, named Jesus. That is an abstract concept. Really young kids, as imaginative as they are, often can't grasp abstract thoughts and conceptualize those into reality. They will learn about Jesus and know answers about Him before they can actually believe and trust in Him. So it's important not to confuse a child who knows things about Jesus and a child who actually places faith in Jesus. Next, a child must know that He was the sacrifice. Whether they articulate this as Christ "dying on the cross for my sins" or "dying on the cross to save us from our sins" isn't the issue. The concept here is substitutionary atonement. It means our penalty was paid for by a suitable substitute. It's not enough to know that Jesus died on the cross. Spiritual transformation comes from understanding WHY. He did not remain dead. He beat death and returned to life.

3. FINALLY, FAITH ALONE IS WHAT SAVES US.

[Ephesians 2:8-10] A lot of people, kids in particular, get caught up in the outward expression of salvation, which is baptism. Eventually, they link that to their actual salvation experience. Baptism does not save anyone. It's basically just a really ineffective bath. We don't even use soap. There is nothing magical about the water. It doesn't wash sins. It doesn't make us official. It's an outward symbol of an inner reality. The biggest red flag that a child is not ready is that they equate becoming a Christian with being baptized. In essence, that is like believing that you become a Christian by going to church or doing good deeds. It's works-based theology incongruent with faith. It's a natural proclivity but it isn't right, so as leaders, pastors, and parents it's really important that we help a child migrate away from thinking that baptism is salvific. The reformers taught us well. *Sola Fide*. Through faith alone.

One key concept that we tend to use as a conversational default, especially with kids, is "asking Jesus to come into your heart." That idea comes from Revelation 3:20. *"Here I am. I stand at the door and knock. If anyone hears my voice and opens the door, I will come in."* It's a beautiful picture of Jesus but not the best concept of salvation, especially for a child. They may articulate Christ coming into their life in those terms and that is fine as long as they also fully understand what it really means to have God in your life. First, forgiveness. A better question for a child to ask Jesus is for his forgiveness. That vernacular indicates an understanding of sin, human need, and a recognition of substitutionary atonement even before they can say or define this term. With kids, it's important to speak in as concrete a language as possible, because they are literal thinkers. Asking Jesus to come into your heart is a great metaphor, but the more literal question is about forgiveness and relationship. It's helpful for us to help them think in those terms. Another concept worth unpacking a bit for them is the idea of becoming a Christian. A better vocabulary is "becoming a Christ-follower." It's semantic for sure, but it helps them understand and reiterate the definition of Christian. It isn't just about being saved from something bad, it's about being saved for something good, to follow Jesus and become like Him.

Overall, this is a lot to handle.

And it should be. Being a Christ-follower is the most important thing about any of us. The decision to follow Christ is just the beginning. Parental goals include the desire to continue helping kids know how to trust and follow God throughout their lives into adulthood. The ultimate goal after spiritual transformation is spiritual maturity. Your spiritual goals are not unlike your other parenting goals. All the things you do for your kids [cooking, laundry, billpay, etc.] are eventually things you have to teach your kids and then release them to do on their own. Following Christ is the same. The goal of teaching them is equipping them. Ultimately, equipping is the core of salvation talks in your family.

"WITHOUT A HEART TRANSFORMED BY THE GRACE OF CHRIST, WE JUST CONTINUE TO MANAGE EXTERNAL AND INTERNAL DARKNESS."

MATT CHANDLER
THE EXPLICIT GOSPEL,
[Crossway, 2014]

Each and every believer should share a common understanding of the atoning sacrifice of Jesus' death on a cross. However, the story of how each and every believer came to know and follow Jesus will vary immensely. Take time in this journal entry to share your own faith narrative. It's your testimony, or the story of how you asked God to forgive your sin and how you trusted Jesus for salvation. While you should also seize any and every opportunity to verbally share this story with your son or daughter, it starts with being able to simply and articulately write down what God has done in your life. Take time to pen that part of your journey.

_____

_____

_____

_____

_____

_____

_____

_____

_____

_____

_____

The further removed we are from significant moments in life, the more fuzzy the details become. Regardless of the age your son or daughter fully experienced God's gift of salvation, their story is part of your story. While it is important that they own and learn how to articulate this crucial component of his or her testimony, you have the perspective of a parent in this moment. Take time to tell your side of the story. When did your child begin seeking, questioning, discovering Jesus? What was the process like? What role did you play in the journey? What did you learn about your own faith in your child's story?

MILEMARKER 4

MATURING

INTRODUCTION TO MATURING

Ah yes...you remember this age, don't you? Strange smells, awkward voice cracks, weird alien-like body behavior, noticing the opposite sex, mood swings strong enough to give any mom or dad whiplash, overuse of the words *like* or *um*...

Adolescence is an important milemarker in the lives of children. It's a stage of development with a lot of changes for you and your child: emotionally, physically, and spiritually. The key word here is "**identity**." Your son or daughter is not only navigating a world of change, but doing his or her best to understand who they are becoming at the same time. No wonder you feel as if you are living with sweet your same sweet child one day and a total stranger the next.

Every day your child will look in the mirror and compare themselves to an unfair, unattainable standard based on others' opinions and mainstream media. Unfortunately, an adolescent's identity is all too easily defined by peers and popular culture.

As a person navigates this stage, the natural reaction is to construct thoughts and learn through experiences. They are in constant eval mode in desperate need of stability. This is a vital time of life for your child to discover his or her own ideas about faith. You cannot miss this stage in preparing your child for their teenage years. Never allow frustration or fear of awkward conversations to keep you from asking questions. As challenging as these years might be, your child is looking for approval and wants answers. If you don't supply them, they'll find them somewhere, possibly in places and people you probably wouldn't approve.

While it's a lifelong process, your objective is to aid your child in establishing his/her identity in Christ. With consistent reinforcement, he/she will have a foundation in Jesus to always lean upon.

QUESTIONS TO CONSIDER AS THEY NAVIGATE THROUGH THIS STAGE:

- Does my son or daughter know that they are beloved?
- What is the most encouraging thing I can say to them today?
- How can I help my child own their faith and value a faith community?

IDEA GENERATOR: How great would it be to walk your preteen through a mission statement for their teenage years? A mission statement is a statement of purpose. For example: My mission is to give my best, serve others, and love God with my actions. Allow your teen/preteen to create their own mission statement to live out. Print it or paint it then frame it and display it as a reminder of who they are becoming in Christ.

FIGHT FOR THE HEART IDOLATRY
[EXODUS 20:3-6, EXODUS 32:22-24]

When the word "idol" or "idolatry" comes up, does your mind immediately go to golden statues and crazy elaborate temples around the world? It's fallacy to believe that as long as we don't bow to inanimate things, idolatry isn't present in our lives. An idol is anything or anyone that takes priority in life over Christ. An idol in life takes/ steals devotion away from God. It would be a lot simpler to identify our idols as statues or temples, wouldn't it?

Moses, one of many heroes in Scripture, had several unusual encounters with God. In one of those moments, God gave him a list of commandments. These commands were meant to help people honor God, but also to reveal human sin and our great need for Him. Do you know commandment number one? It's found in Exodus 20. *"You shall have no other Gods before me."* God immediately addressed idolatry. Why? He knows our hearts are prone to wander. He is a jealous God with no interest in sharing his glory.

Later on, in Exodus 32, we see the same people who had been given the 10 commandments worshipping a handmade golden calf. Seems crazy, doesn't it, to worship an arts and crafts project made out of gold. What? This might sound even crazier, but we have the same tendencies, too. Our hearts are prone to wander just as far, maybe farther. Our idols just look differently, taking many forms, making it more difficult to identify them in our own lives.

Think for a moment: what might be an idol in your life today? (money, career, toys, etc.)

Now, consider the culture your child lives in today. What could be an idol in your child's life?

We live in a world hungry for the attention of children and teenagers. Advertisers specifically market to the younger generation because they know just how influential kids are when it comes to parental attention and especially parental spending. There are many people, ideas, and even items that can take up residence in the hearts of our children--idols that distract them from the life God has planned.

Our job is to identify those idols.

Our job is to protect our children.

It's up to us to fight for their hearts. From the beginning of time, God has been fighting for ours. Despite our constant and often predictable failures, He continues to forgive us and draw us closer. Our role is to do the same for our children.

Despite our constant and often predictable failures, He continues to forgive us and draw us closer.

Think about the word "fight." What emotions are stirred when you think about fighting for your child? What weapons do you have at your disposal? This isn't fighting with your child, although those moments happen in our weakness. This is fighting for your child.

CREATING BOUNDARIES

If you own a piece of property and want to build on it, you have to know the property lines. These boundaries determine where a person can legally place a house, garage, or other desired building project. Building a structure outside of those boundary lines will result in an unpleasant conversation with your neighbors, unfortunate fines, and quite possibly legal action. As frustrating as boundaries may be, our knowledge of those lines will prevent headaches due to unnecessary mistakes.

Boundary lines for Christ-like living are no different. God created boundaries to save us from headaches and unnecessary [even dangerous] mistakes (friendships, dating, sports, cell phone usage, etc…). The good news is those boundary lines have no merit in our salvation. Our salvation securely rests in knowing Jesus Christ [sidenote: "knowing" in Scripture suggests an intimate relationship. Marinate on that as needed]. Biblical boundaries exist to help us live life with character, joy, and honor while we wait for Christ to return.

For the grace of God has appeared that offers salvation to all people. It teaches us to say "No" to ungodliness and worldly passions, and to live self-controlled, upright and godly lives in this present age, while we wait for the blessed hope— the appearing of the glory of our great God and Savior, Jesus Christ, who gave himself for us to redeem us from all wickedness and to purify for himself a people that are his very own, eager to do what is good. -Titus 2:11-14 (NIV)

So…Where do we begin?

BE PROACTIVE IN CREATING A PLAN. Don't be late to the game. The sooner you can talk with your child about boundaries in his/her relationships the better. Boundaries created in the heat of the moment hardly ever result in the behaviors or attitudes you hope to see. For example: Your daughter comes home at 13 and says that she has a boyfriend and they are going to the movies on Friday night. Your reaction to her sudden urge to date may not be pleasant or received well. This might be extreme, but if you fail to have a dating conversation before she begins to be interested in boys, then you have neglected to set clear boundaries for her. How do we create a plan?

BEGIN BY ASKING QUESTIONS.
1. What character traits am I trying to establish within my child?

2. What type of friends do I pray my child finds?

3. How do I protect in certain areas while allowing freedom in others?

BE CLEAR AND EDUCATE.
Plan in hand, you have to communicate it. Being clear on expectations, early on, is crucial. Boundaries don't come naturally. We must educate our kids as to why those boundaries are set. When a child asks "why," the old-school "because I said so" answer is never a good, teachable moment. While obedience without question, regardless of complete comprehension, is an act of biblical submission to God and parents, the Bible is full of explanations. Admit it. Sometimes we default to "because I said so" answers out of laziness, busyness, and even confusion because we're not quite clear ourselves. Use "why" questions to educate and coach your child through the boundaries you've set.

One major aspect of clarity is getting on the same page with your spouse. Even in families experiencing separation or in homes with divorce, a united front in co-parenting is useful. The more divided parents are, the more disruptive a child's behavior can become. The most harmful things when establishing guidelines in friendships, dating, sports, and cell phone usage are unclear boundaries and lack of explanation.

BE IN THE KNOW.

Take time to understand the culture in which your child is growing up. Granted, you can't know everything, but the more you know about your child's culture [their friends, teachers, coaches, social media, and even popular online videos] the better equipped you will be at guiding them through their teenage years. Keep in mind: You will never know what you don't ask. Parents in your circle may not be talking about boundaries until they are beyond necessary. You start the conversation. Be intentional. Get a game plan together before they enter these preteen and teenage years. You and your child will both be grateful you did.

One essential in the life of every Christian is godly accountability. We were never intended to go it alone. Read Hebrews 10:23-25. The purpose of Christian community in those verses is clear. Other verses in scripture provide a distinct harmony across both testaments regarding the importance of accountability in life. For this journal, list the names of various believers at different stages in your life who have held you accountable. Log what was special and beneficial during that season of accountability and the way God used that particular person in your life. Also be prompted to find and establish new layers of accountability in your life currently if you don't have all that you need to remain steadfast in your commitment to Christ as a follower and also as a parent.

_____

_____

_____

_____

_____

_____

_____

_____

_____

_____

Oh the studies that have been conducted. Oh the books that have been written. Everything you want to know about the unique developmental transitions that accompany the physical changes of puberty. Your child is "coming of age" in so many ways during this season. As a journal entry, take time to compose a letter to your son or daughter. Include the following elements:

a. A celebration of who they are and all their unique characteristics and attributes.

b. A note of encouragement indicating the pride you feel being their parent.

c. An admission of your own fear regarding the uncharted waters of this particular season.

d. Your own commitment to being present and purposeful during this next phase. Share with your child your desire to be available, approachable, and flexible.

e. Close with a hopeful word of prayer to be a Christ-like parent raising a Christ-like son or daughter during the preteen and teen years of life.

"YOUR APPROVAL BEFORE GOD IS WOVEN INTO THE LIFE AND SACRIFICE OF JESUS CHRIST ON THE CROSS, NOT WHAT OTHER MEN AND WOMEN THINK ABOUT YOU."

MATT CHANDLER
CREATURE OF THE WORD:
THE JESUS CENTERED CHURCH,
B&H Books, 2012

MILEMARKER 5

FREEDOM

INTRODUCTION TO FREEDOM

In the famous words of William Wallace:
"FREEEEEEEDDDDDOOOOOMMMMM!"

If you've ever seen *Braveheart*, you'll never forget the sound of Mel Gibson shouting those words in his best Scottish brogue. If you happen to be in the .05% of men on plantet earth who haven't seen the film [totally made-up stat], stop now. Go directly to your nearest screen. Don't even waste time on popcorn.

If you listen carefully, on at least one occasion, you can hear every teenager on planet earth belt that same word. Teens long for their parents to step back and provide freedom. They actually need it as part of the developmental process. Freedom is part of maturing. The hard part is defining what freedom actually is and setting healthy boundaries while supporting their need for independence.

The passing of your child into adulthood is a significant process. Biblically, we must equip our children to become men and women of God. The key word at this stage is "**responsibility**." In our culture, age sixteen seems to remain the year teens experience new freedom. It usually comes in the form of keys. But it's more than passing an exam and driving a car.

Teens need to see the importance of their role and responsibility in the Body of Christ, take on the characteristics of Christ, share Christ with their friends, and develop spiritual disciplines. You are his or her primary spiritual leader and you

> You are his or her primary spiritual leader and you have what it takes to help your son or daughter take this next step toward adulthood.

have what it takes to help your son or daughter take this next step toward adulthood.

As you give out responsibility, be careful not to give up important parts of the relationship. Pursue, pursue, pursue. Yes, you want your teenager to mature and begin experiencing life on his or her own to a degree, but the ultimate goal is to find the right pace for those transitions to maintain your connection.

QUESTIONS TO CONSIDER AS THEY
NAVIGATE THROUGH THIS STAGE:
- What are the freedoms you desired as a teenager?
- What freedoms might you extend that are directly tied to greater responsibility within the family?
- Are you giving them opportunities to fail? Or is your fear of giving freedom preventing them from learning and experiencing grace?
- Does your child understand their role in the greater Body of Christ [our local church]?
- How can you continue to encourage servanthood to your child? [hint: saying it is not enough]
- What spiritual disciplines are on display in my life for my child to see?

IDEA GENERATOR: During this stage, kids are typically given keys to a car. Obviously this is a BIG deal. You are now parenting a teenage driver. The tiny baby you swaddled will have *literal* freedom behind the wheel of a moving vehicle. As you hand over keys to a car, what about handing over another set of keys with 10 Bible verses they can carry with them? Choose passages that have offered guidance for you over the years. This will serve as a constant reminder to use their freedom wisely.

PRIORITIES – GREATEST COMMAND
[MATTHEW 22]

In His earthly ministry, Jesus always seemed to be found teaching in the temple courts where he knew the Pharisees and Sadducees would be present. His teachings were aimed to share the good news about the Kingdom of God. More times than not, He was correcting years and years of religious leaders making religion a practice instead of a relationship.

One day, while teaching in the temple courts in Jerusalem, answering questions about the Kingdom of God, Jesus' response silenced the Sadducees (Matt. 22:34). The Sadducees were one of three main Jewish political and religious groups, mainly political. Jesus halted a group of men who almost never ran out of words. Word spread and soon, a young Pharisee showed up to test Jesus. The Pharisees were predominantly religious leaders in nature [far less political] whose primary correlation with the Sadducees was their common disdain for Jesus.

Ok...we must understand something first. The Pharisees claimed to know everything about the law of God. They dedicated their lives to studying and interpreting *Torah* [Old Testament law]. Over centuries, Pharisees added their own set of traditions to God's Word, which is Scripturally forbidden (Deuteronomy 4:2). Their motivation was to protect the law and add layers or hedges around it to keep people from violating it. Pharisees vowed to strictly obey traditions alongside God's law and they enforced this way of life on the Jewish populus.

Think about that for a moment. They not only had to keep up with God's Law, but their own additional rules, totalling well over 600 commands. To say religion was complex is an understatement.

> The first question they asked Jesus makes sense. The young legal expert asked, "Teacher, which commandment in the law is the greatest?" Matthew 22:35-36 (HCSB)

Jesus' response was as fantastic as it was immediate. He didn't quietly ponder and sift through a list of commands to know which one was the most important. He didn't need a bible commentary or a committee to decide. In one sentence, he summed up all commands.

> "Love the Lord your God with all your heart, with all your soul, and with all your mind." Matthew 22:37 (HCSB)

> For good measure, He added a second. "Love your neighbor as yourself." Matthew 22:39 (HCSB)

That's right, to LOVE GOD and LOVE PEOPLE.

As parents, we have the great responsibility to prioritize our family rhythms around what is most important. Like Pharisees, we sometimes have so many things to sift through that matters of great importance become blurry or blended with things of the world. Our busy schedules, sports commitments, investments, careers, etc. leave us asking the question, "what's really the most important?" The heart of the Pharisee's question was, "what matters most?"

The answer is simple.

In your family, is loving God and loving people a noticeable priority? Within your daily routine, even marked on your calendar, while your kids are still under your care, do they know the great emphasis you place on these two? Communication is the burden of the sender and priorities remain the responsibility of parents. If they don't know what Jesus himself deemed as most important, it's up to you to tell them and moreso, to show them.

PETER-FAILURE

Peter, the one Jesus said would begin the church; among the first to answer the call to follow Jesus. Peter, a leader at heart, a man who spoke up and was the first disciple to identify Jesus as the Son of the Living God - the Messiah (Mark 8:29, Luke 9:20, Matt. 16:16-17) Peter, a man's man; a hard-worker, a fisherman by trade, and passionate about his beliefs.

Peter was a man that anyone could look at and say, "that guy is an incredible leader and passionate follower of Jesus." Well...that is, if you decided to skip over a large part of the New Testament. Let's just put things in perspectives shall we...

Peter, although a leader and frequent spokesman for the disciples, often times misspoke. Although he was the first to identify Jesus as the Son of the Living God, he denied Jesus three times in the hour of His greatest need. Peter, though bold, was often in the wrong. In fact, Jesus even called Peter "Satan" at one point after Peter disagreed with Jesus and God's plan for His life (Matt. 16:21-23). When Peter spoke, it was bold. When he erred, it was big.

You see, Peter, while a solid biblical faith hero, was far from perfect. He experienced failure throughout his life, but Peter's failures didn't define him. In all his mishaps and temperamental outbursts, even denying Jesus and downright refusing to accept God's plan, Jesus still used Peter to build His church.

As a parent, remember that your child WILL fail. It is not a question of "if." It's a question of "when." As they do, our response to that failure might be a pivotal moment in their faith journey.

Throughout scripture, God paints a picture of people turning their backs on Him. In return, God invites those same people back into an intimate relationship. Paul writes in the book of Romans, "But God demonstrates His own love for us in this: While we were still sinners, Christ died for us." (Romans 5:8) God is completely justified in punishing our sin. His righteousness earns Him that right. Yet in the same breath, He offers grace by forgiving our sin through the sacrificial death of His Son, Jesus.

God doesn't want failure to define you or dictate your path. He wants Jesus to define you and direct your future. He wants the same thing for your child. WHEN kids fail, we have the opportunity to coach, but we also have an opportunity to love.

WHEN kids fail, we have the opportunity to coach, but we also have an opportunity to love.

HELPING TEENS SEE
A BIGGER PICTURE

Through the years, studies have startled us with stats anywhere from 50-80% of teens who are active in youth groups graduate high school and leave the life of the church all together. While there seems to be an indication that some return later in life, the hiatus is certainly damaging and adulthood is no guarantee that once active teens will come home.

Are you ok with that? You shouldn't be. This is not the vision you have for your child—that after high school, there is an above-average chance he or she will decide to leave the church. You didn't purpose to raise a child that "might" come back. You set out to raise one who doesn't leave. The moment we hear potential pitfalls like these is the moment God births an overwhelming burden. The goal: 0% departure. The goal: children who learn to own their faith, and live their whole life loving God and His church.

Obviously, there are multiple factors contributing. Do young adults see the benefit of the local church? Can they easily identify where to fit in? Have young adults simply lost interest? How are we preparing our kids for life in Christ after they leave home? Without a plan, we plan to fail. We may not bat 100%, but we need a strategy. This is parenting with an end in mind. This is helping your student see the bigger picture of the life God desires for them.

Consider the following ideas and questions about the spiritually successful moments you have witnessed in your son or daughter and even other teens in your church or community.

+ When have I seen my student the most engaged with Christ within their faith journey?
+ When have I seen my church really rally around my student and his overall growth?
+ When have I seen my student living a selfless life and humbly putting God and others first?
+ When have I experienced that same level of Christ-like connection to the church in my own life?

Did you find it? Ultimately, the moments when we see the most selfless, servant leadership and spiritual growth come in seasons where students are actively serving others.

Here's a few things easily observed in students who serve others consistently.

Students who serve...

...activate faith in tangible ways. If our goal is for students to own their faith before leaving us, we must provide opportunities for them to serve others. Faith grows by leaps and bounds through "hands-on" experiences. For students, serving in the church is "on-site" training for a life of faith.

...know where they fit in the local church. When students are afforded the opportunity to serve, the message we send to them is a resounding, "We want you! You are needed and valuable." This is the message we want to send. Students need to know they have a place in the church to use their gifts, talents, and abilities in order to make a kingdom impact. When this happens before graduation, students will know how to fit after matriculation.

...have a bigger perspective of the Church. Students who serve consistently are put in a unique position to put others' needs ahead of their own. We want students to fully understand and own the truth: "Church was never meant to benefit just me. I was designed to participate as part of the we." A bigger picture of the body is a helpful remedy against consumerism and paves the way for a deeper understanding of discipleship.

So...what does this mean for parents? What is your role?

To help students find their place by creating opportunities for them to serve others in order to activate their faith. You've already laid a foundation of biblical truths, now it is time to build on them.

> We have to model for them what we want to see in them.

To model the behavior you want to see. It's the old saying, "don't just talk the talk, walk the walk." Discipleship is far more caught than taught. If your kids never see you serve others, what does this say about the value? Parents, you are the primary influencers in your kids' lives. We have to model for them what we want to see in them.

To fuel the fire. You can't highlight and celebrate enough their efforts to put others first and use their gifts to serve. Popular culture trends toward honoring academics and/or athletics. Make straight A's? Let the celebration begin. Win a football game? Our voice is toast due to all the screaming. These things certainly can and should be celebrated but not at the expense of neglecting more important character-building traits that will ultimately shape life and impact future generations. Parents must ask and answer, "what gets celebrated most in our family?" What we celebrate most tends to be the thing we value most.

To live like Jesus. Goes without saying, right? In your relationships with one another, have the same [sacrificial] mindset as Christ Jesus:

Who, being in very nature God, did not consider equality with God something to be used to his own advantage; rather, he made himself nothing by taking the very nature of a servant, being made in human likeness. And being found in appearance as a man, he humbled himself by becoming obedient to death—even death on a cross! Philippians 2:6-8

Helping teens see the big picture requires effort. It won't happen through osmosis or even a single conversation. It's not even an annual update. If sacrificial serving helps students see a bigger picture, it has to be valued, scheduled, prioritized and repeated within your family. When this happens, you will see a difference in the way you parent, and also the way your child lives.

"HOW YOU EXPRESS AND LIVE OUT YOUR FAITH MAY HAVE A GREATER IMPACT ON YOUR SON OR DAUGHTER THAN ANYTHING ELSE."

KARA POWELL,
STICKY FAITH
Zondervan, 2011

An essential component of the salvation experience is repentance of sin. In order to understand the need for Jesus, a person must come face-to-face with the gruesome reality of his or her sin. Confession and admission of guilt before God is a spiritual discipline and axiom of personal holiness. It's not a one-time sinner's prayer but an ongoing part of discipleship that connects us to our salvation. The way you demonstrate admitting your faults and asking for forgiveness matters to God and it matters to your child. Use this journal prompt to be honest and sincere regarding a personal failure in your life. Know that Christ's forgiveness covers you. Be sure to close with how Jesus responded to your failure and restored you in that moment. In this journal, you are demonstrating the humility you hope to cultivate in your child.

_____

_____

_____

_____

_____

_____

_____

_____

_____

As a parent, you likely long for your child to learn from rather than repeat your mistakes. You also hope that they will model your more successful moments, too. As you grew and experienced more freedoms, you had encounters with both sides of the coin: moments where wisdom prevailed and you exercised good judgment and also moments where you overextended your free will and lived to bear the consequence of your actions. Sharing the former with your child will be far easier than the latter. Fortunately for you, all the gory details of your adolescent mistakes don't need conjuring. How do you know the difference and establish a framework for which details you share and which ones you don't? You need godly perspective and careful planning. Use this journal space to pen your plans for what details to divulge and when/how to divulge them.

_____

_____

_____

_____

_____

_____

_____

_____

_____

_____

_____

_____

_____

_____

_____

_____

_____

_____

_____

_____

_____

_____

_____

_____

_____

_____

_____

_____

_____

MILEMARKER 6

GRADUATION

INTRODUCTION TO GRADUATION

Graduation is finally here! It is bittersweet to say the least. As a parent, you are naturally proud of the many accomplishments your child has made over the years, but at the same time, are more than aware they have grown up and will soon take a giant step into adulthood. This is as unsettling as it is emotional. Have you already begun replaying all the memories? Birth, first day of school, practices and games, first dance, 16th birthday, late night studies, vacations, and much more. Understatement of the century: "Boy, does time ever fly."

Can you remember the day you brought home your bundle of joy? Besides the exhausting feelings of inadequacy, what were your thoughts? What sort of emotions did you feel? Your baby is about to walk across a stage and be handed a diploma steeped in symbolic significance. This is a celebration of 13 years of achievement and also a right of passage into adulthood, taking the next step into manhood or womanhood. Among the many questions running through your head: "Is he ready?" "Can she handle this?" "Have I done enough?"

Parents have the daunting task of preparing a child to leave the comfort of home and face the challenges of the world. Adulthood takes practical skills like being on time, working hard, taking responsibility, cleaning your room, changing a tire, locking up at night, etc. There are spiritual skills to master, too: applying biblical principles, determining the will of God, making wise decisions, owning/sharing/defending faith, giving well, and even the future possibility of marriage and family. The key word for this stage is "**foundation**." Over the course of the past 17 to 18 years you have been laying a foundation for their future.

It is a major misconception that parenting stops when a child graduates. Nothing could be further from the truth, because this is a time when they may need you more. They don't need you to be in their classes or wake them up on time or know every detail of their schedules. [Helicopter alert] They do need you to follow up with them, offer encouragement, answer the phone when they call [even late at night], visit appropriately, and help them identify a church nearby that will help them navigate the next few years entering young adulthood.

QUESTIONS TO CONSIDER AS THEY NAVIGATE THROUGH THIS STAGE:
- How do I help prepare my child for adulthood?
- Does my child know how to articulate their faith?
- Does my child know how to live responsibly and make wise choices?
- How do I let go and remain connected?

IDEA GENERATOR:
Consider the value of a written letter, framed and and given as a keepsake send-off. Call it a "Blessing Letter," written words that allow you to express your deep thoughts and feelings toward your child. It is beyond necessary that you tell them verbally, but what if they carry a concrete example with them to their dorm room or first apartment? We suggest writing qualities you see in your child, dreams you have for their life, encouragement, and a Bible verse to share.

Bonus idea: Over the years, there must have been other adults who made incredible deposits in your child's life. These are people who have partnered with you to lay a faith foundation to prepare them for what is to come. Ask those key adults to write their own notes of encouragement to your child. Collect notes and give them as part of this graduation blessing.

FOUNDATION [COLOSSIANS 2:6-8]

Every year thousands [maybe tens of thousands or even millions] of seniors don cap and gown regalia to walk across stages and receive a diploma signifying the end of high school. This ceremony also represents the beginning of their next step into adulthood, whether that be college or career. At the close, the entire class stands together. In unison, caps go flying through the air like paper airplanes in celebration of a job well done. Honestly, it's as much an achievement for you, the parent, as it is for your hard-working son or daughter. You'll be in the stands smiling proudly with excitement, but maybe also harboring a tinge of sadness. Your baby has grown up. You pray they'll hang on to the faith foundation you established.

In Student Ministry, a particular passage of scripture often comes to mind and is used urge high school seniors/college freshman to be prepared for the persuasions of this world. Everything they know will be tested. Faith will be criticized. The moral compass will be up for examination. For many parents, this is the first time a child has lived away from home for an extended period of time. Just as Paul reminded the early church of their deep roots in Christ, we have to continually remind our children as they step into adulthood.

When Paul wrote to the Colossian church, believers were bombarded with teaching contrary to sound, biblical doctrine. This teaching was a form of Gnosticism [from the Greek word for knowledge] and challenged the basics of Christianity. The biblical foundation that Paul established when he planted the church in Colossae was under scrutiny. Truth was being tested.

"So then, just as you received Christ Jesus as Lord, continue to live your lives in him, rooted and built up in him, strengthened in the faith as you were taught, and overflowing with thankfulness. See to it that no one takes you captive through hollow and deceptive philosophy, which depends on human tradition and the elemental spiritual forces of this world rather than on Christ." (Colossians 2:6-8)

Paul urged the early church to stay centered on Christ and not to be easily persuaded. His solution to this problem? Stay grounded in the faith that was first established in and through Jesus. Ultimately, you desire your kids to own faith before heading out on their own. This means they develop their own personal relationship with Jesus. It means having a faith enhanced by parental influence and family priorities, but ultimately built solidly on Jesus Christ.

As you celebrate this academic milemarker, be certain to celebrate and encourage their faith journey as well. Remind them WHO they are and also WHOSE they are.

This may be the end of their high school career, but it is certainly not the end of your parenting journey. As you let go, you can also lean in. Continue to remind them of their faith in Christ and the grace, love, and purpose found in that relationship. Continue to build on a faith "foundation." It will be a beacon for your emerging adult.

HOW TO PLAN FOR THE NEXT PHASE

If this is your first time parenting an emerging adult you might be asking the question, "what is my next step as my child's parent?" This is a great question and one you should be asking, but know this...you are not alone. Every year high school seniors are looking squarely into the next stage of life. Year after year, parents wonder how to coach/guide and how to let go in order for graduates to learn to navigate life's challenges on their own.

Our goal within this "guide" is to provide just a few ideas to help you prepare your emerging adult for the next part of life. The following six tips can jumpstart how your child may pursue his/her faith before and after leaving your house.

1. Research churches and campus ministries in the area your student could attend. As a parent, helping your child choose a college is incredibly important. College campus tour after college campus tour; you look for the best educational programs, campus safety, best dorm rooms, layout of the campus, and distance from your home. Those are great, but take it a step further. Remember, you may no longer be living in under the same roof, so it is important to discover the people and places that will help build character and spiritual formation. The first two weeks of college for your student are crucial when it comes to their involvement with a local church or campus ministry. Helping your student identify and connect with a local church and campus ministry will offer a great starting point when it comes to a growing faith and engagement in the life of the church.

2. Build confidence for Christianity and biblical worldview through the study of apologetics. Ultimately, the goal is for children to "own" their faith before they leave us. We want them to make their faith personal to them and begin to grow without our prompting. With that said, they will leave your care eventually and listen to many voices outside the protection of your home. This is a good season to build on the foundation you have already set. Another step in owning faith is knowing how to defend faith. The study of apologetics will help your student tremendously. There are several resources you can use. Here's one to try: *Apologetics for a New Generation: A Biblical & Culturally Relevant Approach to Talking About God - Sean McDowell.*

3. Assist in developing or reinforcing basic spiritual discipline practices. Provide the best resources your child will use to encourage spiritual disciples. This development cannot happen without including your child in the process. He/She needs to take the lead with you as their assistant. When you send your child off, you send him/her off with a tool box. That tool box needs to be filled with ways that they can sustain spiritual practices.

4. Stay in touch and facilitate a way for your home church to stay in touch with your student. You may be thinking, "well shouldn't the church leadership find ways to help us with this? Should they just make this happen?" Yes, the church could certainly do a good job following up with college students when they leave, but as their primary spiritual leader you are the facilitator. Don't miss this Lean in...give attention to...and even help the church discover ways to do this for your student along with others.

5. Create a healthy attitude and action plan for doubts about faith and potential moral failures. As your child continues to discover new ideas, they may have doubts about certain aspects of their faith. Be prepared. Just like you go through seasons of life trying to understand the world, your emerging adult will too. Steer clear of judgment, listen to concerns, and encourage. Respond to inevitable mistakes and even moral failure with mercy. Just as Jesus responds to us, extend the grace of our heavenly Father to your child. This doesn't mean that you are condoning behavior or avoiding consequences, but that you are prioritizing the overarching spiritual narrative.

6. Pray. Pray often. Our kids not only need it, but you need it as well. When parents foster a habit of praying and praying often, their trust and faith in God strengthens. He alone holds all things together and all things are through him and for him. (Col. 1:17)

You got this! Keep in mind, the earlier you start this process the better. This is not a study guide to be looked over a week before the final exam. In fact, most of these are just reminders of things you have already been doing. As a parent, you might be quick to say...if he hasn't gotten it by now then he never will; or...it's too late because faith has not been as much as a priority as I would have hoped in my family. It's not too late! You can do this!

Keep in mind that we have a God that is in the business of giving grace, equipping the saints, and giving strength in weakness. The best way you can prepare your child for the next stage in life is to rely on the power of the Holy Spirit through Jesus Christ. The best example of how that is displayed to your child is through you.

This has been quite a journey watching your child grow into the person they are today. You have prayed for and paid for everything in your child's life and now you are sending them off. You have laid a foundation for them and now it is up to them to use that foundation to make decisions in their career choices, relationships, finances, etc. Read Colossians 2:6-8 again. For this journal entry, write down a prayer for your child based on this passage of scripture.

_____

_____

_____

_____

_____

_____

_____

_____

_____

_____

_____

_____

Paul is awarded the lionshare of credit, but he didn't spread the message of Jesus to the Gentile world and change the face of the early church by himself. Even apart from the all-consuming power of God, he had friends. His "thank you" list is long throughout scripture, and in Romans 16 he provides a roll call of men and women who significantly influenced the body. You've heard the phrase, "It takes a village," right? Just how many people have influenced your child's life in Christ? This journal prompt is simple. Take a moment to list the many who have partnered with you in teaching your child over the years. Name and prayerfully thank the adults who have made a profound impact in your child's spiritual/character development.

_____

_____

_____

_____

_____

_____

_____

_____

_____

_____

"EVERY PARENT WILL LEAVE A PERSONAL LEGACY (THOUGH NOT ALL PARENTS WILL LEAVE BEHIND AN INHERITANCE). WHAT I GIVE TO MY CHILDREN OR WHAT I DO FOR MY CHILDREN IS NOT AS IMPORTANT AS WHAT I LEAVE IN THEM."

REGGIE JOINER
THINK ORANGE: IMAGINE THE IMPACT
WHEN CHURCH AND FAMILY COLLIDE,
David C. Cook, 2009

Are you one of those people who skips to the end of a book and reads the last few pages? If you're here on this one, you are one of two people.

You could be this parent: The one who went through each one of these chapters in conjunction with the development of a child. That you? Pause and take a deep breath. Do that awkward arm motion where you attempt to pat yourself on the back. In some ways, you made it. But don't sell the family home and book your ticket to Maui just yet. There is more.

Instead, you could be this parent: The one who read the whole thing cover to cover between feedings. That you? On one hand, it's good that you can check this off your list. On the other, didn't anyone ever tell you to rest while your baby rests? A little shut-eye might have been the more discerning choice at this stage in the game. Nonetheless, you are here, on this page with only a faint image of what this moment could actually look like in your life. Stay the course. This day will come soon enough, and having skipped to the end already, you'll be just that - all ready.

This resource has made no shame regarding our love of all-things Reggie Joiner. Because it makes sense to squeeze one more quote out of him before this work completely ends, take a look at this one:

Never buy into the myth that you need to become the "right" kind of parent before God can use you in your children's lives. Instead learn to cooperate with whatever God desires to do in your heart today so your children will have a front-row seat to the grace and goodness of God.
REGGIE JOINER, THE ORANGE LEADER HANDBOOK, David C Cook, 2010

Everyone knows a couple who waited and waited, pleading with God for the gift of a child. They planned and planned hoping that those plans would somehow, someday, in some way be God's plans for their family. For ease of reading, let's imagine a couple like that and give them names. Marcus and Jamie. Whatever the means, they became parents, great parents. Let's name their son Avery.

Everyone also knows an unexpected, maybe even a very young, single mom. Birth dad checked out. One night. One choice. One moment turned into her forever. Let's do the same and give her an identity. Let's call her Samantha, Sam for short. She was barely 19 when it happened and it actually took longer than average before Sam realized it and came to terms with the reality that she would be a mom. She chose to carry to term and to parent herself. It was rocky and she needed help along the way. We'll give her a little girl, named Violet.

Here's the thing - God planned both. That should go without saying, but sometimes we need a bit of reminding. God wasn't busy doing other things while Marcus and Jamie prayed and cried. He wasn't neglecting His duty as their 100% present and available heavenly Father who delights in giving good gifts. He wasn't relaxing on the other side of the door while biological windows were closing. He planned Avery from the beginning. God picked Avery's birth date. He authored the life of that boy. Avery was worth the wait, worth the prayers, worth the tears.

Similarly, God wasn't falling asleep at the wheel the night Sam conceived. He wasn't surprised or caught off guard. He didn't need a plan B or C when Sam decided to be sexually active. Pregnancy wasn't punishment for sin or a consequence for being irresponsible. Violet was just as planned, just as purposed, and just as [all those

Psalm 139 verses] as Avery. God picked her birthdate, too. Her life is precious.

Let's go a step further. Not only did God create those two kids [well, those fictitious kids in our story, representative of real people in our everyday real world], God also chose those specific parents. Regardless of their personal preparation or lack thereof, God gave those fictitious kids to those fictitious parents.

He gave yours to you, too. Regardless of your readiness. And regardless of the hiccups you have experienced [or will undoubtedly experience] along the way, He planned this family of yours.

Go one step further. He has plans for this family of yours, plans that go well beyond that final graduation milestone. Check out Deuteronomy 6 one more time. This is an important passage so this can't be your last look at Deuteronomy 6, but another reading and deeper explanation is warranted as this word draws to a close.

Hear, O Israel: The Lord our God, the Lord is one. Love the Lord your God with all your heart and with all your soul and with all your strength. These commandments that I give you today are to be on your hearts. Impress them on your children.

Maybe you really are at this transitional moment today. Kids are growing up and leaving home. Empty-nesting is on the horizon. Maybe you still have years to go but like to plan ahead. Final word about parenting? You'll never be finished. Even when your own children are grown, there are more. Without wading into too deep a theological conversation, those words in Deuteronomy 6 weren't only addressed to moms and dads. It was to the whole community of faith. One generation of Israel bore the responsibility of passing faith onto the next generation of Israel. At some point, your responsibility as a follower of Jesus is to come alongside all the Marcuses and Jamies. There are some Sams in your life that need a little of you. Further still, a kid named Avery and a little girl named Violet are looking for some additional adults to help form their understanding of Jesus, to supplement the messages they're getting from home and church, to be part of their faith community.

PASS IT ON

Just because you made it to Milemaker 6 doesn't mean you're done. Until Christ returns, there are miles to go. Journey onward and pass it on.

If your child has indeed turned the tassel and received the piece of paper to prove it, whether you have realized it along the way or not, you have created an incredible resource for your son or daughter. You see, the whole purpose of this Milemarker guide was for you to create a parenting resource of your own to be passed on to your kids. This could be a graduation gift, wedding present, or a legacy gift when your child has a child and you become a grandparent. Crazy to think about, right?

Reflect on all the questions and concerns you had as you awaited your child's arrival. One day, your child might be asking all those same questions. They'll be asking "What do I do?" and "How do I do it?" Through this journal, you've kept a record of the lessons you learned along the way. Lord scripting, one day you might have the opportunity to share the journey you took parenting your son or daughter from birth through graduation. You did it...now pass it on.

YEAR: AGE OF CHILD:

What significant decisions did you make as a parent?

What are the special moments or achievements your child made this past year?

What were some challenges in the past year?

What goals and/or milestones are you looking forward to this year?

YEAR: AGE OF CHILD:

What significant decisions did you make as a parent?

What are the special moments or achievements your child made this past year?

What were some challenges in the past year?

What goals and/or milestones are you looking forward to this year?

YEAR: AGE OF CHILD:

What significant decisions did you make as a parent?

What are the special moments or achievements your child made this past year?

What were some challenges in the past year?

What goals and/or milestones are you looking forward to this year?

YEAR: AGE OF CHILD:

What significant decisions did you make as a parent?

What are the special moments or achievements your child made this past year?

What were some challenges in the past year?

What goals and/or milestones are you looking forward to this year?

YEAR: AGE OF CHILD:

What significant decisions did you make as a parent?

What are the special moments or achievements your child made this past year?

What were some challenges in the past year?

What goals and/or milestones are you looking forward to this year?

YEAR: AGE OF CHILD:

What significant decisions did you make as a parent?

What are the special moments or achievements your child made this past year?

What were some challenges in the past year?

What goals and/or milestones are you looking forward to this year?

YEAR: AGE OF CHILD:

What significant decisions did you make as a parent?

What are the special moments or achievements your child made this past year?

What were some challenges in the past year?

What goals and/or milestones are you looking forward to this year?

YEAR: AGE OF CHILD:

What significant decisions did you make as a parent?

What are the special moments or achievements your child made this past year?

What were some challenges in the past year?

What goals and/or milestones are you looking forward to this year?

YEAR: AGE OF CHILD:

What significant decisions did you make as a parent?

What are the special moments or achievements your child made this past year?

What were some challenges in the past year?

What goals and/or milestones are you looking forward to this year?

YEAR: AGE OF CHILD:

What significant decisions did you make as a parent?

What are the special moments or achievements your child made this past year?

What were some challenges in the past year?

What goals and/or milestones are you looking forward to this year?

YEAR: AGE OF CHILD:

What significant decisions did you make as a parent?

What are the special moments or achievements your child made this past year?

What were some challenges in the past year?

What goals and/or milestones are you looking forward to this year?

YEAR: AGE OF CHILD:

What significant decisions did you make as a parent?

What are the special moments or achievements your child made this past year?

What were some challenges in the past year?

What goals and/or milestones are you looking forward to this year?

YEAR: AGE OF CHILD:

What significant decisions did you make as a parent?

What are the special moments or achievements your child made this past year?

What were some challenges in the past year?

What goals and/or milestones are you looking forward to this year?

YEAR: AGE OF CHILD:

What significant decisions did you make as a parent?

What are the special moments or achievements your child made this past year?

What were some challenges in the past year?

What goals and/or milestones are you looking forward to this year?

About the Authors

Although still navigating the parenting journey themselves, Chase and Nic have a combined 40 years of ministry service with children, students, and families. Leveraging that learning and those relationships, they've created a resource to help parents and caregivers navigate a journey of blessing from the time a child enters the picture until the time they officially set off into adulthood. With degrees in sociology, communication, education, and theology plus too many conference/research learning experiences to count, the goal of this resource is to provide a place to chronicle your own parenting legacy in a thoughtful, Christ oriented way.

Printed in the United States
By Bookmasters